Animal
Antics

Animal Antics

Derek Harvey

SECOND EDITION

Editors Sarah Macleod, Sophie Parkes
US Senior Editor Shannon Beatty
Assistant Art Editor Aishwariya Chattoraj
Project Art Editor Jaileen Kaur
Jacket Designer Brandie Tully-Scott, Dheeraj Arora
Managing Editor Alka Thakur
Managing Art Editor Romi Chakraborty
Producer, Pre-Production Abi Maxwell
Producer Ena Matagic
Jacket Co-ordinator Issy Walsh
Senior Picture Researcher Sumedha Chopra
DTP Designer Dheeraj Singh
Creative Director Helen Senior
Publishing Director Sarah Larter

Consultant John Woodward

This edition published in 2020
First American Edition published in 2014 in the United States by
DK Publishing, 1450 Broadway, Suite 801, New York, NY 10018

Copyright © 2020, 2014 Dorling Kindersley Limited DK,
a Division of Penguin Random House LLC
19 20 21 22 23 10 9 8 7 6 5 4 3 2 1
001-317180-Jan/2020

A catalog record for this book is available from the
Library of Congress.
ISBN 978-1-4654-9243-2

DK books are available at special discounts when purchased in bulk
for sales promotions, premiums, fund-raising, or educational use.
For details, contact: DK Publishing Special Markets, 1450 Broadway,
Suite 801, New York, NY 10018 SpecialSales@dk.com

Printed and bound in China

A WORLD OF IDEAS:
SEE ALL THERE IS TO KNOW

www.dk.com

Introduction

Animals can do the funniest things—even when they don't mean to. Whether they live in forests or deserts, in oceans or on hillsides, all animals have to stay out of danger and find food to stay alive. Jam-packed with funny photographs, Animal Antics provides a snapshot of the crazy world of animals. Who would guess a goat would climb to the top of a tree for its lunch or a giraffe would need to do a split to reach its drinking water? And, it's a good thing there are so many sensible parents around, because baby animals are often the funniest of them all—look out for some naughty little meerkats and a monkey with a snowball!

Family drama

Llama families like to stick together, and take care of their own. However, like any family, they don't always get along...

Llamas are usually friendly and gentle to each other, living in herds mostly made up of mothers and babies, like these two. Sometimes, though, when it comes to proving themselves in the herd, things can get rowdy. From sticking out tongues and spitting, to kicking and biting each other's legs, llamas aren't afraid to do what it takes to be the family favorite.

Snuggle up!

Sometimes we need a little extra help to stay warm—these tiny birds, called bee-eaters, do it by huddling tightly together on a branch.

When they land on their perch, the small birds sidestep along it until they are packed together. A bird on the end looks out for any danger that might come along.

I've got it licked

Have you ever tried to lick your eyeball? It's no problem for the Namib web-footed gecko.

Instead of an eyelid, this gecko has a see-through scale that protects each eye. Living in a dusty desert means the scale gets covered in sand, so what does the gecko do? It licks the scale to clean it!

Large bulblike eyes

Taking cover
Web-footed geckos are covered in pinkish-brown scales that help them blend into their desert surroundings.

Sand swimmers
These small lizards have webbed feet for "swimming" through fine sand.

Web between the toes

Happy in hiding

This three-toed sloth looks happy to be the slowest animal on the planet.

While some animals will try to outrun predators, sloths keep safe by staying still. They move so slowly that jungle predators don't spot them moving in the trees. Their fur is covered in green algae, which also helps keep them camouflaged among the leafy trees.

Want to know a secret?

When you live in a big family group, like these two young meerkats do, it can be tricky to have a private conversation.

Meerkats communicate by using calls, purrs, and other sounds. Different sounds have different meanings, like a warning of danger or a call to go hunting. Some older members of a group can even recognize individuals by their voices.

Having a laugh

Whether you're a human or an ape, like these chimps, there's nothing like joking around with your pals.

Chimps will share jokes with their friends in a group, and even laugh when they are tickled or wrestling with each other. Just like humans, their necks, feet, palms, and armpits are extremely ticklish.

Boo!

This green flower is the perfect place for this striped marsh frog to wait for a mate.

Male marsh frogs attract females with a call that sounds just like a tennis ball being hit. They use their strong front legs to wrestle other frogs to impress the ladies.

Higher!

Sometimes it takes more than a long trunk to stretch for tasty treats in the trees...

By standing on their back legs, elephants can reach very high up. They often have to practice over and over before they can stand like this without losing balance and toppling over.

Splash landing

Even the most skilled surfers sometimes slip up.

Gentoo penguins love surfing the waves in the ocean. To get back on land, they use their powerful flippers to launch themselves out of the water and land on the beach. But sometimes a particularly eager leap, like this one, results in a crash landing!

Turbocharged torpedo
Gentoo penguins are the fastest underwater swimmers of all penguins. They can reach up to 22 mph (36 kmh).

Hold still!

Lynx mothers like their children to be clean and tidy, so will give them a good licking to keep their fur coats looking neat.

Surviving the chilly winters in the far north of Europe, Asia, and North America isn't easy, so lynxes have thick fur that protects them against the cold. Their big, padded toes spread out to help them walk on snow and ice.

I've got my eye on you

When you're this small, finding a hiding place is the best way to avoid bigger, bullying owls.

Boreal owls are one of the smallest types of owls. They live in cold forests close to the Arctic and make their nests in woodpecker holes or nest boxes, like this one, to stay safe.

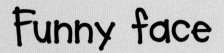

Funny face

This monkey grasshopper looks as though it's been playing with some face paint.

In the sunlight of the tropical forests in the Americas, its bright colors glow like jewels to warn predators. If that doesn't work, its strong legs will help it leap to safety.

Keep smiling!

This playful smile doesn't always mean things are friendly…

Zebras communicate with each other through their loud cry, called a bray. They also make different expressions with their faces. This zebra's toothy grin might look friendly, but it is probably telling others to keep their distance. Full-grown males sometimes fight, but a smile like this could stop it from getting that far.

27

Fasten your seat belts!

Imagine how you would feel with 24 tiny hands and feet clawing at the hair on your back.

Bean-sized possum babies start life inside their mother's pouch and grow quickly by drinking her milk. When they get too big for the pouch, the babies have to get around some other way— they climb onto their mother's back and cling as tightly as they can.

Fancy footwork

Feet this bright are perfect for showing off!

That's just what the male blue-footed booby does to impress the ladies—he struts around waggling his feet. A female booby will choose the male with the brightest blue feet.

Pigging out

A guinea pig's long front teeth never stop growing.

If guinea pigs' teeth didn't grow all the time, they would completely wear down because of all the food they eat. This guinea pig couldn't feast like this if it didn't have teeth!

Silly billies

These goats go to great lengths to reach food in the dry, scrubby lands of North Africa.

Padded hooves help the goats grip the spiky branches of argan trees. They are going after the tasty, olivelike berries that grow on the trees. The goats will attempt to climb even the thinnest of branches to reach the highest fruit.

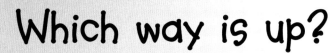

Which way is up?

Like an Olympic gymnast, the Amazon milk frog is a master of spinning around on the slippery stems of jungle plants.

Sticky pads on the tips of their toes help these tree frogs keep a firm grip. Along with their long, strong legs, these toes help them climb high in the rain forest—they even lay their eggs high up in pools of rainwater that have collected in tree hollows.

Look, no paws

This giant panda cub loves hanging around in the trees.

Mothers often leave their cubs alone in the treetops while they go looking for food. Usually the cubs sleep, but tree climbing can be too tempting for some! Pandas sometimes climb as adults too—either to escape danger or simply to sunbathe.

They went that way!

He looks like he's warming up for a boxing match, but this kangaroo is just trying to cool down in the hot Australian desert.

A kangaroo can't sweat to keep cool, so he licks his forearms to coat them with spit. As the spit dries in the sun, it cools his skin and the blood underneath.

Smile for the camera!

For these two young monkeys, a camera is too interesting to ignore.

But don't be fooled by the playful smiles of these crested black macaques from Indonesia... These young pals look like they are grinning at the camera, but a smile like this could actually be a warning!

40

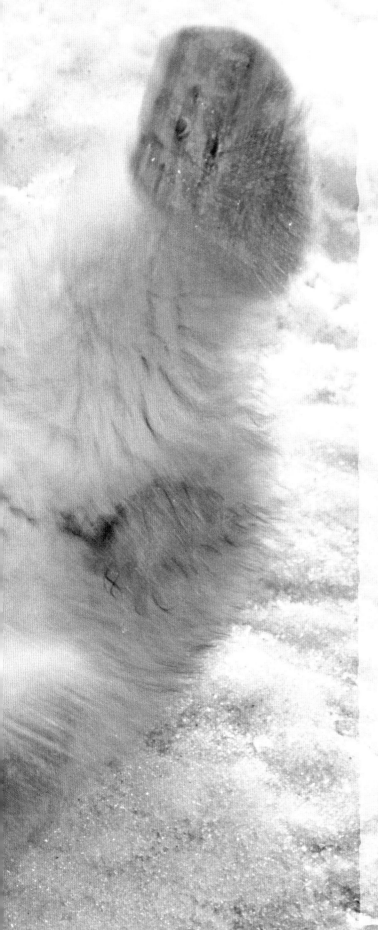

Keeping it clean

How do you get dry when you're surrounded by snow? By rolling around in it, of course.

Polar bears are excellent swimmers and will often travel huge distances in search of food. When they come out of the water they will shake a lot of water off, but will use the snow like a towel to dry themselves, too.

Ears are small to reduce heat loss

A warm fur coat
The polar bear is the world's biggest and heaviest bear. Much of its weight comes from its extra-thick coat, which traps warm air close to the body.

Treading carefully
Big paws are great for walking on slippery snow or paddling through water.

Claws can dig into ice

Balancing act

Could you balance on one leg for more than a minute? This flamingo can do it in its sleep for hours at a time.

A flamingo is most comfortable when standing on one leg with its head and neck flopped across its back. Flamingos rest this way because it takes less effort for their muscles to stand on one leg than to stand on two.

Perfect pouncer

This fox might look like it's entering a diving contest, but that's not why it's plunging into the snow headfirst.

In the winter, when voles and mice are hidden by snow, hunting is tricky for foxes. But their excellent sense of hearing means they can detect tiny rodents scurrying beneath the snow, even when it is 3 feet (1 m) thick. When a fox hears one, it dives right into the snow to grab its dinner.

Kung-fu Komodo

This baby Komodo dragon is doing its best to look scary by standing up and waving its arms like a martial-arts expert.

Young Komodos are good climbers, and spend most of their time in the safety of trees. When they're adults they lose their bright body pattern and turn into huge gray, land-living reptiles: the biggest lizards on Earth.

Swan song

Don't be fooled by a swan's elegance as it paddles across a pond—if you get too close, you could get a nasty peck.

Mute swans are very protective of their babies, called cygnets, and will become aggressive if outsiders come too close. To scare off an intruder, a swan will hiss, charge, peck, and even whack them with their huge wings!

Super snoozer

You would find it much too chilly to sleep in the Arctic, but a walrus can nod off just about anywhere—on land and in the water.

Walruses have even been seen snoozing while hanging onto the side of an ice sheet by their tusks! They need to doze whenever they can, because some walruses have been known to swim for more than 80 hours at a stretch.

Mucking around

On Africa's grassy plains, this white rhino and its calf love nothing more than frolicking in the mud.

When you live in a hot climate, finding a way to keep cool is a must. White rhinos will lie in the shade or wallow in the mud of a water hole to escape the searing heat. The mud is more than just a cooler—it acts as insect repellent and sun protection, too.

Bear behind

This bear cub looks like it's playing hide-and-seek, but it's actually getting ready to shimmy up this tree.

Young brown bears are able to climb trees, but when they get older they become too heavy. Instead, adults spend all their time on the ground. It's a useful fact to remember if you ever need to escape an adult!

I didn't do it!

Who is guilty of gobbling a large hole in this leaf?

On this occasion, the katydid (a type of cricket) peering through the nibbled hole is not guilty—it looks like the culprit was actually a hungry snail.

To the beach

Gray seals are often seen chilling out on the beaches of the northern Atlantic Ocean.

They spend a lot of time in the water, where they are strong swimmers. They chase different kinds of fish and eat up to 11 lb (5 kg) of food a day. During the winter, they spend more time on land, where their heavy bodies make them clumsy.

Heads down

A giraffe's long legs and neck are great for reaching treetop treats, but they do make it pretty hard to have something to drink.

Thirsty giraffes have to stand with their legs far apart, like they're trying to do a split, so that their head can reach the water. Strong muscles push water up the neck into the stomach.

Amazing ant–ics

Human weight lifters can lift nearly twice their own weight, but that's nothing compared to an ant.

These tiny red ants carry these fruit buds all the way back to their nest where they will feed their colony. Each bud is only the size of a peppercorn, but 50 times the weight of an ant. Sticky pads on their feet stop them from falling as they balance.

Puffed out

It looks like it's going to be a bumpy landing for this Atlantic puffin returning from a fishing trip!

A hefty haul of sand eels will be the perfect feast for its chicks. While they make their home on the tops of rocky cliffs during breeding season, puffins spend most of their lives at sea. They use their wings to "fly" through the water, diving as deep as 200 ft (60 m) to catch their fish dinner.

Look both ways!

Is this chameleon looking up or down? Actually, it's doing both!

Chameleons' eyes can move separately from each another—one eye can point one way while the other looks in a different direction. Each eye is able to swivel almost 180 degrees—great for spotting juicy insects.

Catching some zees

If you ever spot a koala in a tree, chances are it will be snoozing.

Koalas eat the leaves of eucalyptus trees. The leaves are very tough and it takes a long time for koalas to digest them. The best way to help their body break down the leaves is to take a nice long nap while they go down!

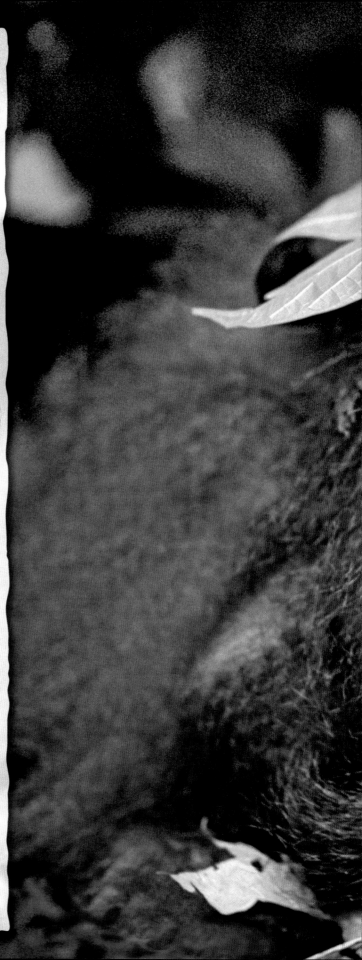

Under my umbrella

When your fur is as fabulous as this, you have to use what you can to keep it dry when there's a rain-forest downpour.

Young orangutans stay with their mothers for as long as seven years—longer than any other type of ape. They learn all the skills they will need to survive, such as how to use a leaf as an umbrella!

Hands are like those of humans, but have longer fingers

Toes can curl to grip objects

King of the swingers
Orangutans have extremely long arms but their legs are short and stumpy. This means they feel more at home climbing and swinging through trees than walking on the ground.

Get up and boogie

Polar bears look pretty big on four legs—never mind on just two!

Standing tall helps a polar bear scare off threats, see farther across the Arctic landscape to look for food, and smash through the snow to find baby seals underneath to eat. At its full standing height of more than ten feet (3 m), the polar bear is the world's largest land-living carnivore.

Cuddle up

The cuddly capybara is the biggest rodent on Earth.

These creatures are very good swimmers. A strong, pig-shaped body and partly webbed feet are perfect for paddling, and their long fur is designed to dry out very quickly on land. Female capybaras raise their young in groups and protect them from predators on land and in the water.

Bandit country

In grassy areas in North America, called prairies, an underground burrow makes the perfect lookout for these young black-footed ferrets.

The ferrets' parents stole this burrow from a colony of prairie dogs, a type of large ground squirrel. The ferrets raised their family here, and used the prairie dogs for food. When the young ferrets grow bigger they will move into neighboring burrows.

Parallel parking

You need a good grip when you spend your life scrambling through bushes.

Like all insects, a praying mantis has six legs. It uses four of them for holding onto stems and twigs. Armed with powerful claws, the front pair of legs is used to grab passing prey.

Who says I'm scary?

This jaguar didn't just heard a funny joke. It's snarling to reveal its terrifying teeth.

Jaguars are the top predators in the Amazon rain forest. Among the trees, their patterned coats are excellent camouflage for creeping up on prey such as forest pigs and deer.

Three's a crowd

What's the smallest space you have ever squeezed your body through? It won't beat that of the house mouse.

House mice have such tiny bones that they can squeeze through spaces the width of a pencil. If their heads get through, then their flexible bodies will, too. Mice nest under floorboards in houses, emerging at night to eat, leaving behind tiny droppings and nibbled packages of cookies!

Hoo-hoo are you?

This burrowing owl is looking at life from a different angle.

In grassy areas of South America, an owl living on the ground needs to keep an eye out for danger. It twists its flexible neck to get a good angle for spotting a tasty mouse or a dangerous predator. Long legs help it to chase rodents, but also to see above the long grass where it makes its home.

Lion dancing

These lions look like they are rehearsing a rumba, but they are really just honing their hunting skills.

Play is an important part of growing up if you're a young lion. Play fighting teaches these two cubs how to control their movements so that one day they can catch prey.

Pucker up

You would be forgiven for thinking that this creepy creature had been playing with some lipstick!

The red-lipped batfish is a very unusual fish. Its disk-shaped body is not much good for swimming, so it chooses to waddle along on the ocean floor instead and "stand" using its stiff fins as "legs." It isn't fast enough to chase other fish to eat, so it uses a long body part that extends from the top of its head to attract its dinner.

Eat your greens!

This wolf cub is learning the hard way that wolves don't normally eat grass.

At just nine weeks old, this wolf cub knows very little about the big wide world and relies on its parents for protection and food. For now, it will spend its time playing near the den, before joining the grown-ups on hunts when it gets bigger.

Long legs for running

When I'm calling you...
Adult wolves howl loudly to bring the pack together. They can be heard from several miles away.

Fast foodies
Wolves have sharp teeth and a strong bite. They eat fast before other predators steal their kill.

Nose can pick up distant scents

Run for cover

The beach is no fun in the rain, especially when you have babies to take care of. With no other shelter, there is only one option…

This plover must brave the bad weather while her chicks snuggle in her belly feathers to keep warm and dry. She can fit as many as four chicks beneath her. Luckily the rain will bring worms to the surface to make her struggle worth it!

Who's laughing now?

**Like humans, chimpanzees use their faces
to show how they are feeling.**

Chimp expressions do not always mean the same thing as ours,
though. When a chimp bears its upper teeth and gums, it is not
amused, but nervous or aggressive. If its jaw drops to show the
lower teeth, like a human frown, the chimp is in a good mood.

Nice catch!

A long beak might be handy for reaching food—but you need the skills of a juggler to get it down your throat.

A toucan tosses fruit into the air to swallow it. Although the toucan's beak looks heavy, it is actually very light and tough because it is made from thin strands of bone arranged like a sponge. The outer layers are made of a substance called keratin, which is also found in hooves and nails.

When you gotta go...

In the forests of Borneo in Southeast Asia, a pitcher plant makes the perfect outhouse for a tree shrew.

Pitcher plants are carnivorous plants with pitchers that grow from the end of their leaves. Each pitcher contains liquid to drown insects, whose bodies feed the plant. But the tree shrew also plays a part—as it eats the plant's nectar, it uses the pitcher as a toilet, and its poop provides vital nutrients for the plant.

Hanging around

These baby opossums love the thrill of dangling from a branch.

For now, they can use their hairless tails like an extra limb to hold on to their perch, but this fun won't last. As they get older, they'll grow too heavy for their tails to support them this way.

A prickly situation

Have you ever regretted a decision? This bobcat probably did when it came face-to-face with a cougar and escaped up this cactus.

With a cougar hot on its tail, the bobcat had to get to a safe place as quickly as it could. A spiky cactus probably wasn't the most comfortable perch for it to choose, though...

Don't let go!

At just two weeks old, baby harvest mice are already ace acrobats.

A harvest mouse can use its tail to grasp twigs or hang upside down just for fun. Harvest mice are the smallest rodents in Europe—even when it is fully grown, one could sit comfortably in a teaspoon.

Three little pigs

These young wild boars haven't been sipping a frothy drink—they have actually been snuffling in the snow in search of food.

Wild boars are experts at sniffing things out—they start rooting around when they are just a few days old! They'll search for all kinds of tasty things, from wiggling worms to acorns.

Yogi bear

Big paws are great for getting food, fighting off danger, and also for just rolling around!

Brown bears, whether children or adults, can be very playful. They are curious creatures which will check out any new noise, smell, or object they come across to see if they can eat or play with it. Most bears live alone, but they do form friendships with other bears nearby.

Brown bears have a noticeable shoulder hump

Long claws are ideal for digging

Flat-footed plodders
Brown bears have flat feet, like humans. They are good for supporting weight, but not as good for speed, so bears can't run as fast as animals like dogs and cats, which walk on their toes.

It's nippy out!

This thumb-sized crayfish has its very own built-in suit of armor.

These crayfish normally spend the day in the safety of a muddy burrow—but sometimes they are caught in the open. When danger comes along, they stand as tall as they can and wave their pincers in the air. If anyone comes too close, they might get a nasty nip. Even baby crayfish have to fend for themselves—a strong pair of pincers certainly helps.

Glorious mud

An African elephant loves nothing more than playing around in the mud.

Elephants coat themselves with wet mud because it cools the body down as it dries—lifesaving in the baking hot sun of Africa. First the elephant sucks the mud into its trunk, then it blows a spray of mud at the hottest parts of its body!

Feeling crabby

This crab from Hawaii holds a pretty pair of poms-poms in its claws.

The pom-poms are tiny sea creatures called anemones. The anemones have stinging tentacles to scare off predators. The tentacles also trap bits of food, so the pom-poms are not just for defense but for dinner, too.

Leap frog

Long, springy legs are ideal for practicing gymnastics.

Red-eyed tree frogs spend most of their time climbing in trees instead of hopping on the ground. Their green skin blends in well with their leafy surroundings. But if they are spotted by a predator, a quick flash of those bright red eyes is often enough to scare them off.

I'm bushed!

There's nothing better than stretching out on a branch for a catnap after a long day of hunting.

No other big cat is as at home in the trees as the leopard. When the expert climber makes a kill, it uses its great strength to drag the carcass up into a tree. Here, it hides the prey in the leaves, far from the attention of other predators who might try to steal its prize.

Paws for thought

Ready for a quiet snooze, this sleepy sea otter covers its eyes to help it doze.

Sea otters spend most of their time in the cold ocean—they even sleep there. Unlike other sea mammals, sea otters don't have much fat under their skin, so they rely on their fur to stay warm. Their coat has more hair than any other mammal and it must be kept spotless to keep the cold out.

Sashaying sifaka

This prancing primate moves from tree to tree with the grace of a ballet dancer.

As it crosses open ground by hopping sideways on two legs, this sifaka holds its arms stretched out for balance. The silky-haired creature from Madagascar is named for the call of "shi-fak" that it makes as it leaps through the trees.

Feed me!

You'd need a big net to catch the number of fish that a pelican can catch in its pouch.

When the pelican scoops below the water's surface, the large, stretchy pouch which hangs from its beak collects a load of fish. The water drains over the sides, and the pelican swallows the fish whole. Although they usually eat fish, pelicans have been known to try turtles, frogs, and even pigeons.

Call of the wild

This marmot looks as though it's bursting into song, but it's more likely to be a male defending his domain.

Standing up on his back legs, he makes a loud warning call to protect his territory, females, and family from other males that might invade.

Beach gymnastics

How flexible are you? Elephant seals are so limber that when they curl up they can touch their tail to their nose.

A flexible spine means this seal can twist and turn quickly in the water, helping it chase and catch fish to eat. Adults spend most of their time in the water. They can dive to great depths and hold their breath for more than an hour.

Sensitive whiskers help seals sense prey

Speedy swimmer
The streamlined shape of a seal is ideal for underwater swimming. With no ear flaps, its head is perfectly smooth.

Perfect paddlers
On land, its flippers are no good for walking, while in the water, they are used to steer.

There are nails at the end of the flippers

Old bug-eyes

This tiny tree climber might look like a big-eyed goblin, but it is a relative of monkeys and humans.

The tarsier uses its extra-large eyes to spot insect prey at night in the rain forest. Each eye is as big as its entire brain, and takes up so much room in the head that they are fixed in position—this means the tarsier has to twist its whole head around to look in a different direction.

Dress to impress

Do my antlers look big in this? The bigger the better for this red deer.

To show off, male red deer thrash the undergrowth with their antlers, building up strength in their neck muscles. This strength becomes useful in winning antler-to-antler battles with other males to impress the females.

Snake in the sand

For a snake in the open desert, the dry sand makes an ideal hiding place for an ambush.

This horned adder buries itself in sand, where it can sense the movement of lizards scampering on the surface. When a lizard comes close enough, the adder shoots its head out to grab its dinner.

I've got this ball!

For this mouse, an old, worn-out tennis ball makes the perfect home.

This harvest mouse would usually build its nest from a bundle of shredded grass attached high up on a reed, but a tennis ball is much safer. The hole the mouse has made is big enough to let the mouse in, but small enough to keep hungry weasels and birds of prey out.

118

The perfect partner!

How do penguins brave freezing cold Antarctic winters? By finding a great mate!

Emperor penguins raise chicks in some of the worst conditions imaginable. They put possible mates to the test by acting things out with them. This includes preening each other's feathers—especially the parts that are hard to reach—and mirroring each other's movements, like this pair.

Happy feet

Penguins' feet don't freeze because their bodies have an incredible system which keeps them at a temperature just warmer than freezing at all times.

Claws stop them from slipping on ice

Natural blanket

Penguin feathers are very short to help them swim, but they are tightly packed together to keep them warm.

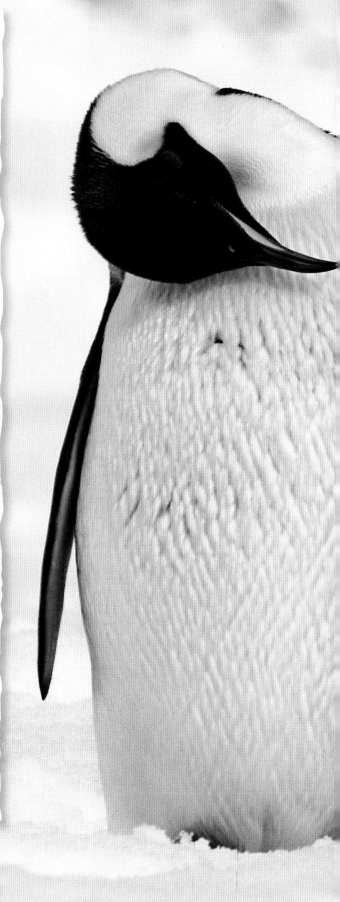

Feeling shy

Hiding behind a reed, this damselfly would be hard to spot if it wasn't for its bulging, blue eyes.

Its long wings can lie flat along its thin body, hidden from predators. When it needs to eat, the damselfly flutters over ponds in bright sunlight, using its huge eyes to spot and snatch other insects in flight.

Can you do this?

Doing a split between two reeds is no problem for this blackbird.

The female red-winged blackbird is quite relaxed as she grasps her perches. Here, she will build her nest above the water, safely hidden from predators among the reeds, and in the company of a lot of other females of her kind.

Gorilla-back ride

This little gorilla is tired out after a long day of playing in the trees and chasing friends.

Gorillas and humans have a lot in common, which is not surprising since they're our close cousins. These great apes are friendly, intelligent, and emotional, showing feelings such as sadness, joy, and love. Like humans, gorillas take care of their young for the first few years of their life, providing food, protection, and even transportation!

Where'd it go?

A newborn kangaroo is incredibly small—barely the size of a peanut.

The baby, called a joey, has a lot of growing to do before it can survive on its own, so it stays safe inside its mother's pouch for the first four months of its life. Here, the mother feeds it with her rich milk and keeps checking that her baby is doing well.

Down came a spider...

With its long, thin arms, legs, and tail, you can see how the spider monkey got its name.

At first glance, the tail of this spider monkey looks like an extra arm, since it is used to grab branches. At the tip, a patch of bare skin works like a sensitive fingertip to get a better grip—very handy for swinging through the trees.

Don't touch!

This critter looks cute, but if you pick it up, you'll get a prickly surprise.

Hedgehogs are covered in about 6,000 hard hairs called spines. When threatened by a predator—or a human doing some gardening—the long-eared hedgehog will run away or curl up into a ball. Curling up makes its sharp spines point outward, turning back anyone who comes too close.

Fill it up!

Even with its cheeks chock-full, this chipmunk can't resist a few more nibbles of a cracker.

Surviving cold winters when it is too cold for food to grow can be tough for the chipmunk. So, instead of eating all its food at once, it collects some of its food in its large cheek pouches, and carries it back to its burrow to store it for winter.

Flying floor mop

Is it a bird? Is it a plane? No—this shaggy animal is a dog with dreadlocks.

The Puli is a type of sheepdog with an amazingly thick, waterproof coat that forms long, ropelike cords. Despite their heavy coat, Pulis can move very quickly and easily and can change direction in an instant when chasing intruders.

Bouncing baby

It's not only human kids that enjoy tumbling around—bonobo youngsters do too.

Bonobos are apes that are closely related to human beings. They live only in the forests of central Africa in large, friendly groups. Some scientists think that bonobos are particularly good at understanding how other members of the group feel, and will do what they can to keep everyone happy.

Sticking your neck out

If you had a long, powerful neck like this, you would want to show it off.

When male giraffes fight, they do it in style. With their front legs spread wide for balance, each giraffe swings its head and neck to smash into the other. Fighting can last for half an hour before the weakest finally gives up. The winner becomes the top male, which means he is more likely to get a mate and become a father.

Singing in the rain

Using a leafy umbrella to shelter from the rain, this frog is about to make an important call.

During a downpour, a male red-eyed tree frog will call loudly to attract a female. When they have found each other, she will give him a piggyback ride for a few hours until they are ready to lay eggs. They lay them on a leaf that hangs over a pool of water so that when the eggs hatch, the tadpoles inside fall into the water and live there until they become frogs.

Having a ball

It's unusual to see monkeys in snow, but if you go to the far north of Japan you might catch them.

Japanese macaques have shaggy coats to keep them warm in a place that is icy cold for a lot of the year. In the coldest winters, they huddle for extra heat. The cold doesn't stop the youngsters from getting into mischief—this playful monkey can't resist starting a snowball fight!

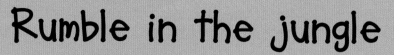

Rumble in the jungle

If two chameleons come face-to-face on a small twig, who gets right-of-way?

Unlike these young chameleons, adults have a colorful body pattern, with spots or stripes of yellow and blue. The colors get brighter when they get excited or angry, such as when they get into arguments with other chameleons. Without the bright colors, these young chameleons will just have to do their best to look mad.

Dozing off

This fluffy red panda looks surprisingly comfortable curled up on a tree branch.

Red pandas are excellent climbers and spend most of their time in the trees, even sleeping high up in the branches. While their thick red fur with white markings looks as though it would stand out, it actually camouflages the pandas, since these trees are often covered with red-brown moss and white lichen.

Index

Acknowledgments

Dorling Kindersley would like to thank Clare Joyce for design assistance; Susmita Dey and Seeta Parmar for editorial assistance; Claire Bowers and Romaine Werblow for picture research; Ann Baggaley for proofreading; and Jane Perlmutter-MacPherson for Americanization.

The publisher would like to thank the following for their kind permission to reproduce their photographs:
(Key: a-above; b-below/bottom; c-center; f-far; l-left; r-right; t-top)

4-5 Dreamstime.com: Ksenia Raykova (c). **6-7 Dreamstime.com**: Espoir2004. **8-9 Photoshot**: Martin Harvey / **NHPA. 10-11 National News and Pictures. 12-13 Getty Images**: Art Soul Photography. **13 naturepl.com**: Hermann Brehm. **14-15 Getty Images**: Luke Horsten / Moment. **16-17 Getty Images**: Juergen + Christine Sohns / Picture Press. **18 Caters News Agency**: Steven Passlow. **19 Corbis**: David Fettes. **20-21 Getty Images**: Andy Rouse / The Image Bank. **21 Dreamstime.com**: Martingraf (crb). **22-23 Dreamstime.com**: Marina Cano. **24 Alamy Images**: blickwinkel / Peltomaeki. **25 Alamy Images**: Photoshot Holdings Ltd. **26-27 Getty Images**: Heinrich van den Berg. **28-29 Alamy Images**: Rick & Nora Bowers. **30 Dreamstime**.com: Kseniya Ragozina (bl). **30-31 Dreamstime.com**: Martinmark (bc). **31 Dreamstime.com**: Kseniya Ragozina (br). **32-33 Getty Images**: Picture by Tambako the Jaguar. **34-35 Getty Images**: Perry McKenna Photography / Moment. **36-37 FLPA**: Artur Cupak / Imagebroker. **38 Corbis**: Mitsuaki Iwago / Minden Pictures. **39 Corbis**: Jami Tarris. **40-41 naturepl.com**: Anup Shah. **42-43 Corbis**: Alaska Stock. **44-45 Dreamstime.com**: Sergey Kovalev. **46 Corbis**: Robert Postma / First Light (c). **47 Getty Images**: Robbie George / National Geographic (bc). **48 Caters News Agency**: Woe Hendrick Husin. **49 Alamy Stock Photo**: Steve Taylor ARPS. **50-51 Corbis**: Alaska Stock. **52-53 Dreamstime.com**: Simon Eeman. **54 Solent Picture Desk**: Valtteri Mulkahainen. **55 Caters News Agency**: Steven Passlow. **56-57 Corbis**: Hinrich Baesemann / dpa. **58-59 Corbis**: Denis-Huot / Hemis. **60-61 Caters News Agency**: Eko Adiyanto. **62-63 Alamy Stock Photo**: Wild Dales Photography - Simon Phillpotts. **64 Getty Images**: Jack Milchanowski / age fotostock. **65 Dreamstime.com**: Ongchangwei. **66-67 Corbis**: Anup Shah / Nature Picture Library. **68 naturepl.com**: Steven Kazlowski (bc). **68-69 naturepl.com**: Steven Kazlowski. **69 naturepl.com**: Steven Kazlowski (bc). **70-71 Getty Images**: Joe McDonald / Corbis Documentary / Getty Images Plus. **72-73 Getty Images**: Wendy Shattil and Bob Rozinski / Oxford Scientific. **74 naturepl.com**: Michel Poinsignon. **75 Getty Images**: Ammit. **76-77 Alamy Images**: blickwinkel / Delpho. **78 Solent Picture Desk**: Henrik Nilsson. **79 Solent Picture Desk**: Jacques Matthysen. **80-81 Getty Images**: Birgitte Wilms / Minden Pictures. **82 Dorling Kindersley**: Jerry Young (bl). **Dreamstime.com**: Sean Donohue (cl). **82-83 Getty Images**: Art Wolfe / The Image Bank. **84-85 Solent Picture Desk**: Michael Millicia. **86 Corbis**: Dlillc. **87 Corbis**: Dlillc. **88 Getty Images**: Visuals Unlimited, Inc. / Gregory / Visuals Unlimited. **89 FLPA**: Chien Lee. **90-91 Corbis**: Ronald Wittek / dpa. **92 Solent Picture Desk**: Curt Fohger. **93 FLPA**: J.-L. Klein and M.-L. Hubert. **94-95 Alamy Images**: Willi Rolfes / Premium Stock Photography GmbH. **96-97 FLPA**: Andre Skonieczny,I / Imagebroker. **97 Dreamstime.com**: Isselee (crb). **98-99 FLPA**: Jasper Doest / Minden Pictures. **100-101 Corbis**: Anup Shah.

102 Alamy Images: David Fleetham. **103 Caters News Agency**: Mercury Press. **104-105 Robert Harding Picture Library**: Morales / age fotostock. **106-107 Ardea**: Tom + Pat Leeson. **108 Robert Harding Picture Library**: imageBROKER (tl). **108-109 Robert Harding Picture Library**: Michael Runkel. **109 Robert Harding Picture Library**: Arco Images. **110 Getty Images**: Susan Freeman / Flickr. **111 Alamy Images**: Juniors Bildarchiv / F275. **112-113 Robert Harding Picture Library**: Michael Nolan. **114-115 Dreamstime.com**: Vitaly Titov & Maria Sidelnikova. **116 Solent Picture Desk**: Greg Morgan. **117 Corbis**: Martin Harvey. **118-119 Corbis**: Roger Tidman. **120-121 Robert Harding Picture Library**: Michael Nolan. **122 Solent Picture Desk**: Tony Flashman. **123 Corbis**: Arthur Morris. **124-125 Getty Images**: Art Wolfe / Stone. **126 FLPA**: D. Parer & E. Parer-Cook. **127 SuperStock**: Minden Pictures. **128-129 Getty Images**: Vyacheslav Oseledko / AFP. **130 Dreamstime.com**: Bruce Shippee. **131 Alamy Images**: Wegler, M. / Juniors Bildarchiv GmbH. **132-133 Corbis**: ZSSD / Minden Pictures. **134-135 Dreamstime.com**: Mogens Trolle. **136 Getty Images**: Michael Durham / Minden Pictures. **137 Getty Images**: mochida1970 / Moment Open. **138-139 Dreamstime.com**: Cathy Keifer. **140-141 Alamy Stock Photo**:Juniors Bildarchiv GmbH. **141 PunchStock**: Digital Vision / Keren Su. **142-143 Fotolia**: Eric Isselee (tc)

Cover images: *Front:* **Dreamstime.com**: Photka c; **iStockphoto.com**: GeorgePeters / E+; *Back:* **Alamy Stock Photo**: Wild Dales Photography - Simon Phillpotts ca; **Depositphotos Inc**: ammmit cb; **Dreamstime.com**: Anna Moskvina crb; *Spine:* **Dreamstime.com**: Martinmark t

All other images © Dorling Kindersley
For further information see: **www.dkimages.com**